MAKE IT!

Moving Machines

Anastasia Suen

Rourke
Educational Media

rourkeeducationalmedia.com

- duct tape
- electric toothbrush
- glue (optional)
- Lego axle and wheel
- Lego bricks
- Lego person
- littleBits battery unit
- littleBits blue power module
- littleBits green DC motor (tethered) module
- littleBits green fan module
- littleBits motor mate
- littleBits mounting board
- markers
- newspaper to cover the work area
- paint
- paintbrush
- pencils
- pipe cleaners (optional)
- plastic bottle with cap
- plastic eyes (optional)
- plastic lid
- pool noodle (with hollow center)
- round lids (1 large, 1 small)
- rubber bands
- ruler
- sand, snow, water, or ice
- scissors
- single-hole punch
- Styrofoam tray
- water table, kiddie pool, or large plastic bin

Table of Contents

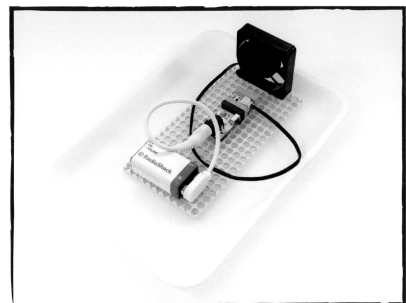

Moving Machines

Jumping, spinning, twisting, turning, racing—the power is in your hands. Use **energy** to make machines that move!

Make bots that jump and spin. Build a rubber band racer and a bottle boat. Power a boat and a car with air.

Art Bot

YOU WILL NEED:

- electric toothbrush

- AA batteries

- rubber band

- 4 markers

- pool noodle (with hollow center)

- scissors

- ruler

- plastic eyes (optional)

- glue (optional)

- pipe cleaners (optional)

Tip:

Buying an inexpensive electric toothbrush with a motor inside usually costs less than buying the motor by itself.

BUILD A ROBOT THAT MAKES ART!

Here's How:

1. Turn on the toothbrush to test the batteries. (Replace if needed.)

2. Cut five inches (127 millimeters) off the pool noodle.

3. Decorate the small noodle. Draw a face with markers.

Tip:
You can also glue on plastic eyes and add pipe cleaner hair.

4. Push the brush inside the noodle.

5. Push part of the handle into the noodle.

6. Keep on/off switch above the top of the noodle.

Tip:

If the toothbrush can move back and forth in the noodle before you turn it on, wrap paper around it to make it fit snugly.

on/off switch

7. Wrap a rubber band around the noodle.

8. Place the markers inside the rubber band. Make them into legs.

9. Remove the marker caps.

10. Turn on the toothbrush. Place your art bot on a sheet of paper and watch it go!

Why Does It Work?

The art bot moves because the toothbrush moves back and forth. It vibrates. Energy caused by movement is called **kinetic** energy.

Spinning Bot

- 9-volt battery

- littleBits battery unit

- littleBits blue power module

- littleBits green DC motor (tethered) module

- littleBits motor mate

- Lego bricks

- Lego axle and wheel

- Lego person

- 3 rubber bands

- large sheet of paper

- marker or crayon

BUILD A SPINNING ART BOT.

Here's How:

1. Begin with the power source. Connect the white battery cable to the 9-volt battery. Look at the terminals carefully. Snap the opposites together.

2. Plug the battery cable into the blue power module.

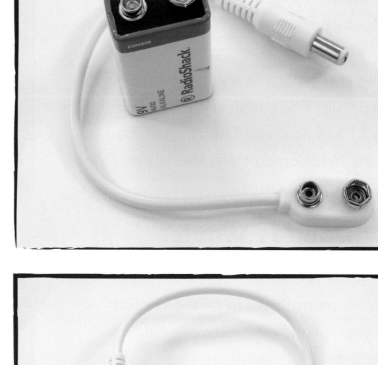

Tip:

The small round snap is the positive terminal. The wide tall snap is the negative terminal.

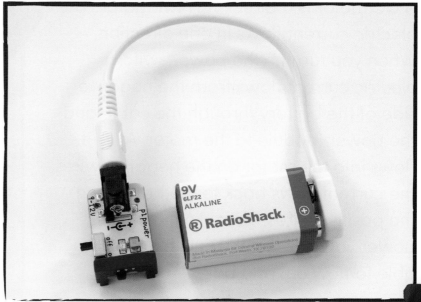

3. Snap the green DC motor (tethered) module magnet to the blue power module magnet.

4. Flip the switch in the blue power module. If the battery is still good, the light will turn on. The motor shaft will turn. Your **circuit** will be ready. (If not, use a new battery.)

Why Does It Work?

A DC motor is a direct **current** motor. The electric current flows in one direction. When you turn on the power switch, electric current flows from the negative side of the battery through the cable and the power module to the motor. After it flows into the motor on the negative wires, the current flows back to the battery on the positive wires. To make the circuit power your device, the current must be able to flow out and back.

Tip: The littleBits modules connect to one another with magnets. If a module is facing the wrong way, the magnets will not connect.

5. Turn off the switch. Make a platform of Lego bricks longer than the battery. Place the circuit on the Lego. Click the module feet into the Lego.

6. Now make a stack. Put the white motor module shaft on the table.

7. Place the DC battery on top of the white motor module shaft.

8. Stack the Lego platform on top of the battery. Hold the stack together with rubber bands.

Tip: Wrap one rubber band around the front of the stack. Then wrap another rubber band around the back of the stack.

9. Place a white motor mate on the DC motor shaft.

10. Attach a Lego axle to the other side of the motor mate.

11. Add a wheel to the axle.

12. Build a Lego chair in the back for the driver.

13. Wrap a new rubber band around the cable and a marker.

14. Take off the marker cap and turn on the power.

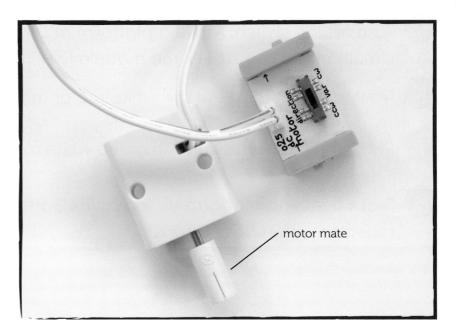

motor mate

Why Does It Work?

The art bot spins in circles because there is only one wheel. Moving back and forth isn't the only kind of kinetic energy. Going in circles is called **rotational** movement.

Rubber Band Racer

MAKE A RACE CAR POWERED BY RUBBER BANDS.

Here's How:

1. Trace a large lid on the cardboard twice. Cut out the two back wheels.

2. Trace a small lid on the cardboard twice. Cut out the two front wheels.

3. Use a sharp pencil to poke a hole in the center of each wheel.

Tip:
Paint the race car after you cut out all four wheels.

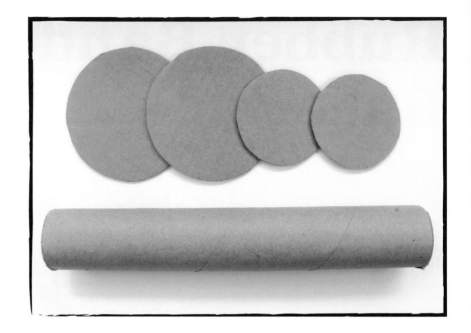

4. Make a hole for the axle. Push the pencil through the hole.

5. Mark the spot for the hole on the other side. Then punch a hole for the other axle.

6. Repeat to make axle holes on the back of the tube.

7. Wiggle the pencil in all four holes to make them wider.

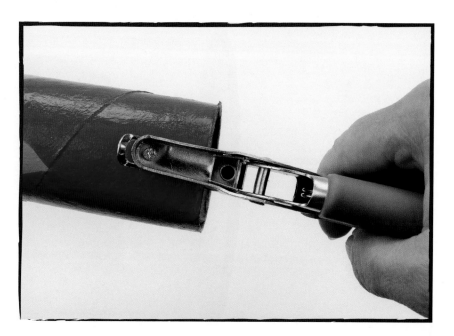

Tip:

If the axle holes are too tight, the axle will not turn freely.

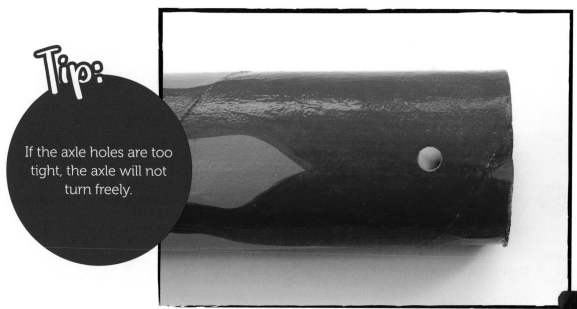

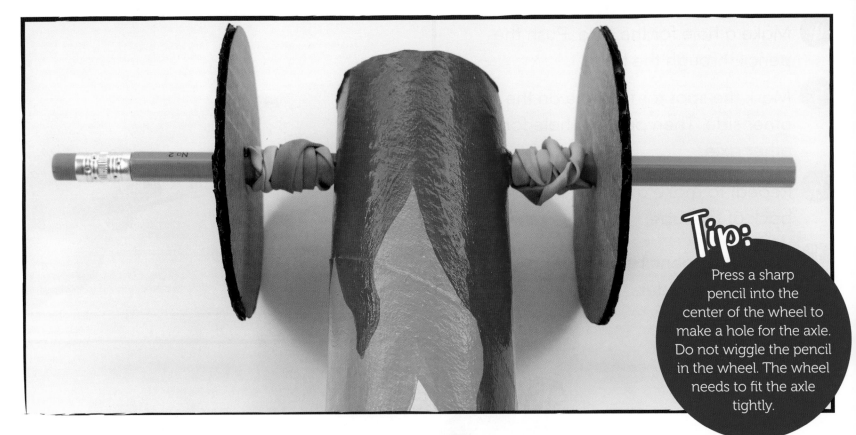

Tip:

Press a sharp pencil into the center of the wheel to make a hole for the axle. Do not wiggle the pencil in the wheel. The wheel needs to fit the axle tightly.

8. Put the first small wheel on the pencil axle.

9. Wrap a rubber band around the pencil near the wheel.

10. Poke the pencil through the first axle hole.

11. Wrap another rubber band around the pencil.

12. Put the second wheel on the pencil.

13. Repeat for the large back wheels.

14. Make a rubber band chain.

15. Wrap the rubber band chain around the rear axle.

16. Add a paper clip to the end of the chain. Drop the paper clip into the tube.

Tip: To make a rubber band chain, put one rubber band on top of another. Lift the bottom rubber band up and pull it back through itself to make a knot. Repeat until the rubber band chain is longer than the tube.

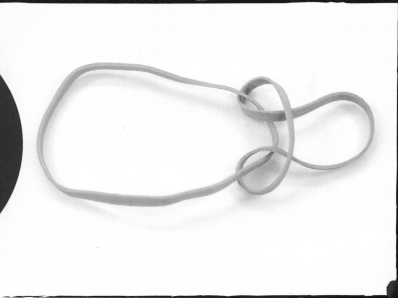

19

17. Turn the tube around. Cut two short slits in the bottom of the tube.

18. Remove the paper clip. Pull the rubber band into the front slits.

19. Turn the back wheels to wind up the rubber band.

20. Put the car on the floor and let it race!

Why Does It Work?

Twisting the back wheels to wind up the rubber band creates **potential** energy. It creates energy that is waiting to be released. When the car is placed on the floor, the rubber bands unwind, making the car move. Potential energy turns into kinetic energy.

Tip:

Place the rubber band chain under the front pencil axle.

Bottle Boat

YOU WILL NEED:

- plastic bottle with cap

- 2 pencils

- duct tape

- rubber bands

- plastic lid

- water table, kiddie pool, or large plastic bin

- water

POWER A PLASTIC BOTTLE BOAT WITH A PROPELLER.

Here's How:

1. Tape a pencil on each side of a plastic bottle.

2. Stretch a rubber band between the pencils.

3. Cut a plastic lid into a rectangle. This is the propeller.

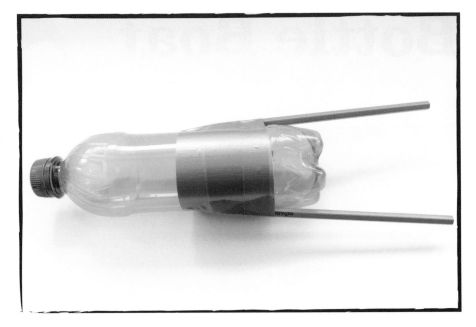

Tip:

If one rubber band isn't long enough, make a chain.

4. Staple the plastic lid to the rubber bands.

5. Turn the propeller around several times to wind up the rubber band.

6. Put the boat in the water and let go of the propeller.

Tip:

Staple the middle of the propeller across the rubber band two or three times. Add more staples above and below the rubber band.

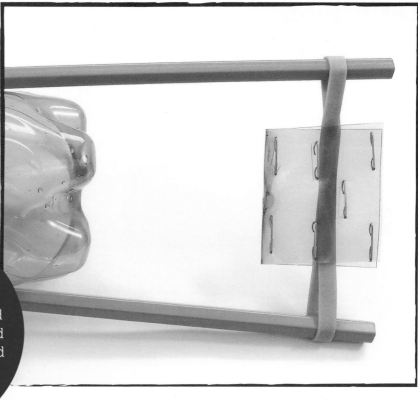

Why Does It Work?

Winding the rubber band gives the boat potential energy. The more times the rubber band is wound, the more potential energy it has.

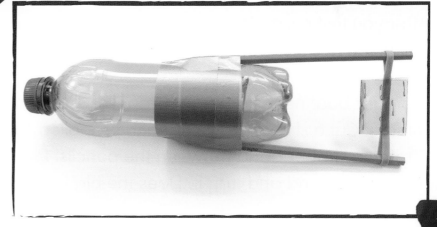

Go Bigger

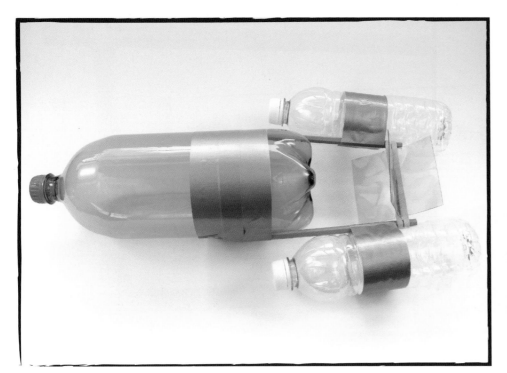

After you test a simple propeller model, build a bigger one. Use a two-liter bottle for the main hull in the middle. Tape a small bottle to each pencil for side hulls.

A bigger boat needs a bigger propeller. Cut two plastic rectangles and draw a line in the middle. Cut a slit halfway into each propeller. Turn one over and fit the two cuts together. Stretch a rubber band between the pencils. Place the big propeller between the two sides of the rubber band and turn it. Does the big boat go faster than the smaller one?

Air Power

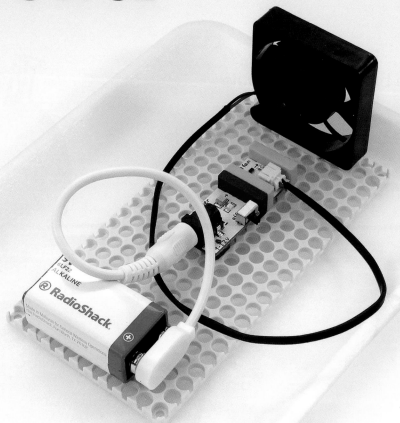

YOU WILL NEED:

- 9-volt battery

- littleBits battery unit

- littleBits blue power module

- littleBits green fan module

- littleBits mounting board

- Styrofoam tray

- water table, kiddie pool, or large plastic bin

- sand, snow, water, or ice

25

MAKE A BOAT POWERED BY AIR.

Here's How:

1. Connect the battery to the blue power module.

2. Add the green fan module to the blue power module.

3. Turn on the power to test the battery.

Tip:

If the battery is still good, the power light will turn on and the fan will spin. Your circuit is ready. If it doesn't work, replace the battery.

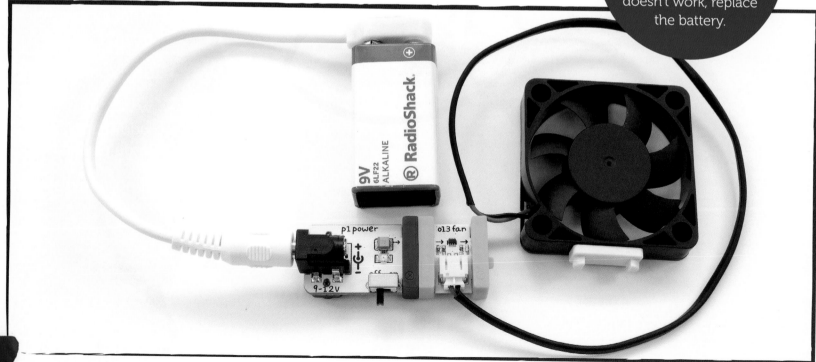

4. Turn off the power. Disconnect the battery cable.

5. Put the mounting board on the table.

6. Place the fan at the back of the board.

7. Press the circuit onto the board.

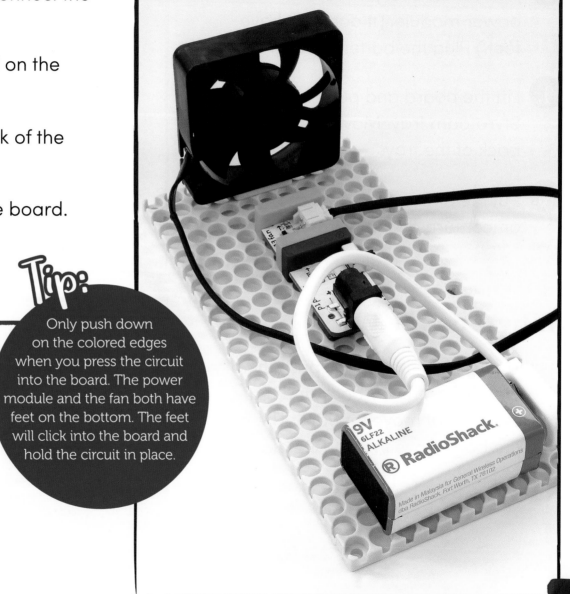

Tip:

Only push down on the colored edges when you press the circuit into the board. The power module and the fan both have feet on the bottom. The feet will click into the board and hold the circuit in place.

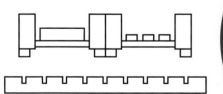

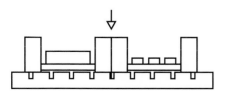

8. Place the battery in front of the power module. (It does not have feet.) Plug the battery cable in again.

9. Lift the board and put it in the Styrofoam tray. Move the fan to the back of the tray.

10. Put the airboat on sand, snow, water, or ice. Turn on the power and let go!

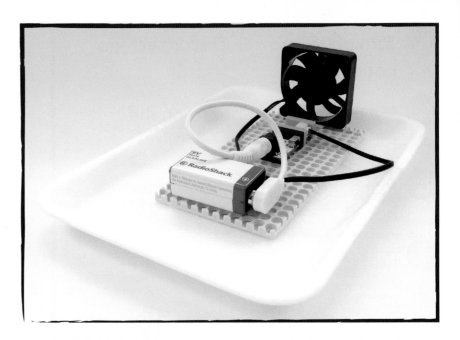

Why Does It Work?

As the fan spins, the blades push the air. The fan pushes the air back and that makes the boat move forward. The air and the boat move in opposite directions.

It's a Boat! It's a Car!

Airboats can travel on sand, snow, water, or ice because they are flat on the bottom. Early airboats had airplane engines to turn their propellers. Today, most airboats have car engines.

You can use your airboat circuit board to power a car made of Legos or K'NEX. Make a flat bed with axles and wheels underneath. Use littleBits brick adapters to connect the Lego to the board. For a K'NEX car, pull twist ties or pipe cleaners through the holes on the corners of the board.

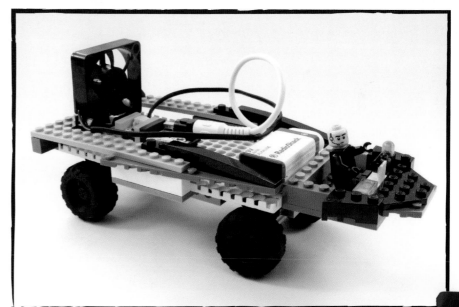

29

Glossary

circuit (SUR-kit): a complete path that electricity can flow on

current (KUR-hent): the movement of electricity in a wire

energy (EN-ur-jee): power from a battery or another source, like a rubber band unwinding

kinetic (ki-NET-ik): movement

potential (puh-TEN-shuhl): something that is possible in the future, like the energy from a wound-up rubber band

rotational (roh-TAY-shuh-nuhl): turning around like a wheel on an axle

Index

Show What You Know

1. Why do you only push part of the toothbrush handle into the pool noodle?

2. Describe how a circuit powers your device.

3. How do you make a chain with rubber bands?

4. Why do you twist the rubber band chain?

5. Explain how a fan makes a machine move.

Websites to Visit

http://littlebits.cc/tips-tricks/tips-tricks-littlebits-lego

http://littlebits.cc/projects/c-robot

http://dnr.wi.gov/topic/WardenWire/WardenWire_Lookup.asp?id=239

About the Author

Anastasia Suen is the author of more than 250 books for young readers, including *Wired* (A Chicago Public Library Best of the Best Book) about how electricity flows from the power plant to your house. She reads, writes, and edits books in her studio in Northern California.

Meet The Author!
www.meetREMauthors.com

www.rourkeeducationalmedia.com

PHOTO CREDITS: Cover, Backcover, & Pages 4–29: © creativelytara; Backcover: © kyoshino; Page 9: © Rebbeck_Images; Page 28: © Aneese; Page 29: © Jackasbati

Edited by: Keli Sipperley
Cover and Interior design by: Tara Raymo • CreativelyTara • www.creativelytara.com

Library of Congress PCN Data

Moving Machines / Anastasia Suen
(Make It!)
ISBN 978-1-68342-379-9 (hard cover)
ISBN 978-1-68342-888-6 (soft cover)
ISBN 978-1-68342-545-8 (e-Book)
Library of Congress Control Number: 2017934540

Rourke Educational Media
Printed in the United States of America,
North Mankato, Minnesota